Make in a
Weekend Shawls

by Jean Leinhauser
and Rita Weiss

Leisure Arts, Inc.,
Little Rock, Arkansas

Produced by

Production Team

Creative Directors: Jean Leinhauser
and Rita Weiss

Senior Technical Editor: Ellen W. Liberles

Editor: Susan Lowman

Pattern Tester: Susan Jeffers

Photographer: Carol Wilson Mansfield

Book Design: Linda Causee

Published by Leisure Arts

© 2013 by Leisure Arts, Inc.,

5701 Ranch Drive

Little Rock, AR 72223

www.leisurearts.com

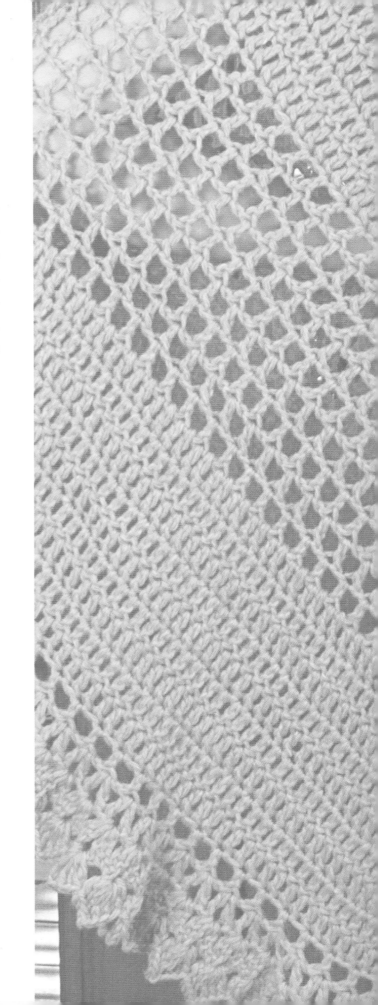

INTRODUCTION

Need a quick shawl to make a fashion statement or to wrap someone special in your prayers and friendship? You're sure to find a design that's just right in this creative crochet collection. The 12 designs offer a wide array of looks for all ages—even toddlers!

Lacy styles crocheted with medium or bulky weight yarn, each one can be made in just a weekend. Of course, a "weekend" can mean many things—from the standard Friday night to Monday morning, to a four-day holiday weekend, to a lengthy "lost" weekend where you settle in and really get lost in your work.

But whether you can finish in just a few hours, a few days, or even a few weeks, it's of little importance. Making a shawl should be a pleasure. It's not necessary to race the clock. There is no prize for the one who finishes first. So long as you put a little bit of yourself into all of your stitches, the results will be the same: a beautiful shawl to wear with a smile or to wrap around someone who needs a warm hug!

SHELL SENSATION SHAWL

A simple shell shawl decorated with a lovely collar and warm thoughts can bring smiles to the recipient.

Skill Level: Intermediate ■■■□

DESIGNED BY MARGARET HUBERT

Size

Approximately 33" long x 68" wide
  (84 cm x 173 cm)

Materials

Worsted weight yarn

[100% acrylic, 5 ounces, 256 yards (140 grams,
  234 meters) per skein]

  3 skeins lavender (A)

  1 skein green (B)

  1 skein turquoise (C)

Note: *Photographed model made with Red Heart® Soft
Yarn® #3720 Lavender (A), #9522 Leaf (B) and #2515
Turquoise (C).*

Size K (6.5 mm) crochet hook (or size required for
gauge)

2" (5 cm) diameter button of choice

Stitch markers

Gauge

5 shells = 6" (15 cm)

6 rows = 4" (10 cm)

Stitch Guide

Beginning shell (beg shell): Ch 3, 2 dc in first
dc: beg shell made.

Shell: (Sc, ch 3, 2 dc) in specified ch-sp: shell
made.

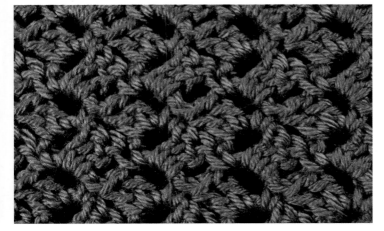

Starting at bottom back point, with Color A,
ch 3.

Row 1 (right side): Work 2 dc in 3rd ch from
hook (shell made): 1 shell; turn.

Row 2: Work beg shell, shell in beg ch-sp on
Row 1: 2 shells; turn.

Row 3: Work beg shell, shell in ch-sp of first
shell, shell in ch-sp of beg shell: 3 shells;
turn.

Row 4: Work beg shell, shell in ch-sp of first
shell, shell in next ch-sp, shell in ch-sp of beg
shell: 4 shells; turn.

Row 5: Work beg shell, shell in ch-sp of first
shell; *shell in next ch-sp; rep from * across
to beg shell, shell in ch-sp of beg shell: 5
shells; turn.

Rep Row 5, 52 more times: 1 more shell in
each row (57 shells at end of Row 57). At end
of Row 57, do not turn and do not finish off.

EDGING

Working along side edge, shell in each ch-3
sp across to bottom point of shawl, shell in
point, shell in each ch-3 sp across to top corner of shawl; join with sl st in first dc of beg
shell on Row 57. Finish off; weave in ends.

instructions continued on page 6

COLLAR

With Color A, ch 119.

Row 1: Work 2 tr in 6th ch from hook (skipped chs count as separate first tr); *skip next 2 chs, 2 tr in next ch; rep from * across to last 3 chs; skip next 2 chs, tr in last ch: 38 groups of 2 tr and 1 tr at each end; ch 1, turn.

Row 2 (right side): Note: *Work first scallop from top of post to bottom and next scallop from bottom to top of post to form a wavy row around neck, alternating direction for each scallop made.* Skip first tr, (sl st, ch 3, 5 dc) around post of next tr, 6 dc around post of next tr (scallop made), skip next 2 tr; *(6 dc around post of next tr) twice (scallop made), skip next 2 tr; rep from * 17 times more; dc in first skipped ch at beg of Row 1 (in first tr): 19 scallops and 1 dc. Finish off Color A; weave in ends. Turn.

Row 3: With wrong side facing, join Color B with sl st in same ch as last dc worked on Row 2 (in first tr on Row 1), ch 3 (counts as first tr); *2 tr in sp between next 2 tr on Row 1; rep from * across to last tr; tr in last tr: 38 groups of 2 tr and 1 tr at each end: ch 3 (counts as dc on next row), turn.

Row 4: Skip first tr; *skip next 2 tr, (6 dc around post of next tr) twice; rep from * 18 times more; sl st in top of beginning ch-3: 19 scallops and 1 dc. Finish off Color B; weave in ends. Turn.

Row 5: With wrong side facing, join Color C with sl st in top of beg ch-3 on Row 3, ch 3 (counts as first tr); *2 tr in sp between next 2 tr on Row 3; rep from * across to last tr; tr in last tr: 38 groups of 2 tr and 1 tr at each end; ch 3 (counts as tr on next row), turn.

Row 6: Rep Row 2, working last dc in top of beginning ch-3 on Row 5: 19 scallops and 1 dc. Finish off Color C; weave in ends.

FINISHING

Place markers at center of top edge on shawl and at center of last row on collar. With right side of shawl and wrong side of collar facing, pin last row of collar to top edge of shawl, matching marked center points. Sew collar in place.

BUTTON AND CLOSURE

Join Color A with sl st to top edge of shawl at right edge of collar, ch 50. Finish off; weave in ends. Sew button to top edge of shawl at left edge of collar. Wrap chain around button to form closure.

BLOCKING

Place shawl on a padded surface. Sprinkle with water, pat into shape and allow to dry.

The Faroese Shawl

Wrap a happy lady in this traditional design from the Faroe Islands where the distinguishing feature of their shawls is that lovely center back gusset shaping.

Skill Level: Intermediate ◼◼◼◻

DESIGNED BY CHERI MCEWEN

Size

Approximately 30" long x 64" wide
(76 cm x 163 cm)

Materials

Worsted weight yarn

[100% wool, 3.5 ounces, 220 yards (100 grams, 202 meters) per skein]

      4 skeins orange

Note: *Photographed model made with Cascade 220 Heathers, #2451*

Size I (5.5 mm) crochet hook (or size required for gauge)

Gauge

13 dc = 4" (10 cm)

7 dc rows = 4¼" (11 cm)

Stitch Guide

V-stitch (V-st): Work (dc, ch 2, dc) in specified st or sp.

2 dc decrease (2-dc dec): *YO, insert hook in next st and draw up a lp, YO and draw through 2 lps on hook*, skip next st; rep from * to * once; YO and draw through all 3 lps on hook: 2-dc dec made.

3 dc decrease (3-dc dec): [YO, insert hook in next st and draw up a lp, YO and draw through 2 lps on hook] 3 times, YO and draw through all 4 lps on hook: 3-dc dec made.

Shell: Work (2 dc, ch 2, 2 dc) in specified st or sp.

Large shell (lg shell): Work (3 dc, ch 2, 3 dc) in specified st or sp.

instructions continued on page 9

INSTRUCTIONS

Row 1 (wrong side): Beginning at neck edge, ch 4 (counts as dc), (dc, ch 2) 3 times in 4th ch from hook, 2 dc in same ch: 6 dc and 3 ch-2 sps; ch 3 (counts as dc on next row now and throughout), turn.

Row 2 (right side): Dc in next dc, ch 2, dc in next ch-2 sp, ch 2, V-st in next ch-2 sp, ch 2, dc in next ch-2 sp, ch 2, dc in last 2 dc: 8 dc and 5 ch-2 sps; ch 3, turn.

Row 3: Dc in next dc; *ch 2, dc in next ch-2 sp, dc in next dc, dc in next ch-2 sp, ch 2**; 3 dc in next dc, ch 2, 3 dc in next dc; rep from * to ** once; dc in last 2 dc: 16 dc and 5 ch-2 sps; ch 3, turn.

Row 4: Dc in next dc; *ch 2, dc in next ch-2 sp, dc in next 3 dc, dc in next ch-2 sp**, work (ch 2, 2 dc in next dc, dc in next dc, 2 dc in next dc) twice; rep from * to ** once, ch 2, dc in last 2 dc; 24 dc and 5 ch-2 sps; ch 3, turn.

Row 5: Dc in next dc; *ch 2, dc in next ch-2 sp, 2 dc in next st, dc in next 3 sts, 2 dc in next dc, dc in next ch-2 sp, ch 2**; †dc in next dc, 2-dc dec over next 3 sts, dc in next dc††; ch 2, V-st in next ch-2 sp, ch 2; rep from † to †† once, then rep from * to ** once; dc in last 2 dc: 30 dc and 7 ch-2 sps; ch 3, turn.

Row 6: Dc in next dc; *ch 2, dc in next ch-2 sp, 2 dc in next dc, dc in next 7 dc, 2 dc in next dc, dc in next ch-2 sp, ch 2**; 3-dc dec, ch 2, 3 dc in next dc, ch 2, 3 dc in next dc, ch 2, 3-dc dec; rep from * to ** once; dc in last 2 dc: 38 dc and 7 ch-2 sps; ch 3, turn.

Row 7: Dc in next dc; *ch 2, dc in next ch-2 sp, 2 dc in next dc, dc in each dc across to last dc before next ch-2 sp, 2 dc in next dc, dc in next ch-2 sp, ch 2**; skip 3-dc dec; †2 dc in next dc, dc in next dc, 2 dc in next dc††; ch 2; rep from † to †† once; skip 3-dc dec; rep from * to ** once; dc in last 2 dc: 48 dc and 5 ch-2 sps; ch 3, turn.

Row 8: Dc in next dc; *ch 2, dc in next ch-2 sp, 2 dc in next dc, dc in each dc across to last dc before next ch-2 sp, 2 dc in next dc, dc in next ch-2 sp, ch 2**; †dc in next dc, 2-dc dec over next 3 sts, dc in next dc††; ch 2, V-st in next ch-2 sp, ch 2; rep from † to †† once, then rep from * to ** once; dc in last 2 dc: 54 dc and 7 ch-2 sps; ch 3, turn.

Row 9: Dc in next dc; *ch 2, dc in next ch-2 sp, 2 dc in next dc, dc in each dc across to last dc before next ch-2 sp, 2 dc in next dc, dc in next ch-2 sp, ch 2**; 3-dc dec, (ch 2, 3 dc in next dc) twice, ch 2, 3-dc dec; rep from * to ** once; dc in last 2 dc: 62 dc and 7 ch-2 sps; ch 3, turn.

Rows 10 through 18: Rep rows 7 through 9 three more times: 24 more dc in each row than in 3 rows back (example: 24 more dc in Row 9 than in Row 6). At end of Row 18: 134 dc and 7 ch-2 sps; ch 3, turn.

Row 19: Dc in next dc; *ch 2, dc in next ch-2 sp, 2 dc in next dc, ch 1, skip next dc, (dc in next dc, ch 1, skip next dc) across to last dc before next ch-2 sp, 2 dc in next dc, dc in next ch-2 sp, ch 2**; skip 3-dc dec; †2 dc in next dc, dc in next dc, 2 dc in next dc††; ch 2; rep from † to †† once; skip 3-dc dec; rep from * to ** once; dc in last 2 dc: 84 dc, 5 ch-2 sps and 60 ch-1 sps; ch 3, turn.

instructions continued on page 10

9

Row 20: Dc in next dc; *ch 2, dc in next ch-2 sp, 2 dc in next dc, ch 1, skip next dc, (dc in next dc, ch 1, skip next ch) across to last 3 dc before next ch-2 sp, dc in next dc, ch 1, skip next dc, 2 dc in next dc, dc in next ch-2 sp, ch 2**; †dc in next dc, 2-dc dec over next 3 sts, dc in next dc††; ch 2, V-st in next ch-2 sp, ch 2; rep from † to †† once, then rep from * to ** once, dc in last 2 dc: 86 dc, 7 ch-2 sps and 64 ch-1 sps; ch 3, turn.

Row 21: Dc in next dc; *ch 2, dc in next ch-2 sp, 2 dc in next dc, ch 1, skip next dc, (dc in next dc, ch 1, skip next ch) across to last 3 dc before next ch-2 sp, dc in next dc, ch 1, skip next dc, 2 dc in next dc, dc in next ch-2 sp, ch 2**; 3-dc dec, (ch 2, 3 dc in next dc) twice, ch 2, 3-dc dec; rep from * to ** once; dc in last 2 dc: 90 dc, 7 ch-2 sps and 68 ch-1 sps; ch 3, turn.

Row 22: Dc in next dc; *ch 2, dc in next ch-2 sp, 2 dc in next dc, ch 1, skip next dc, (dc in next dc, ch 1, skip next ch) across to last 3 dc before next ch-2 sp, dc in next dc, ch 1, skip next dc, 2 dc in next dc, dc in next ch-2 sp, ch 2**; skip 3-dc dec; †2 dc in next dc, dc in next dc, 2 dc in next dc††; ch 2; rep from † to †† once; skip 3-dc dec; rep from * to ** once; dc in last 2 dc: 96 dc, 5 ch-2 sps and 72 ch-1 sps; ch 3, turn.

Rows 23 through 27: Rep Rows 20 through 22 once, then rep Rows 20 and 21 once: 12 more dc and 12 more ch-1 sps in each row than in 3 rows back.

Row 28: Dc in next dc; *ch 2, dc in next ch-2 sp, 2 dc in next dc, dc in each dc and ch-1 sp across to last dc before next ch-2 sp, 2 dc in next dc, dc in next ch-2 sp, ch 2**; †2 dc in next dc, dc in next dc, 2 dc in next dc††; ch 2; rep from † to †† once, then rep from * to ** once; dc in last 2 dc: 216 dc and 5 ch-2 sps; ch 3, turn.

Rows 29 through 31: Rep Rows 8 and 9 once, then rep Row 7 once.

Row 32: Dc in next dc; *ch 2, dc in next ch-2 sp, 2 dc in next dc, dc in each dc across to last dc before next ch-2 sp, 2 dc in next dc, dc in next ch-2 sp, ch 2**; †dc in next dc, 2-dc dec over next 3 sts, dc in next dc††; ch 2, dc in next ch-2 sp, ch 2; rep from † to †† once, then rep from * to ** once; dc in last 2 dc: 245 dc and 6 ch-2 sps; ch 3, turn.

Row 33: Dc in next dc; *ch 2, dc in next ch-2 sp, 2 dc in next dc, dc in each dc across to last dc before next ch-2 sp, 2 dc in next dc, dc in next ch-2 sp, ch 2**; 3-dc dec, ch 2, 3 dc in next dc, ch 2, 3-dc dec; rep from * to ** once; dc in last 2 dc: 251 dc and 6 ch-2 sps; ch 3, turn.

Row 34: Dc in next dc; *ch 2, dc in next ch-2 sp, 2 dc in next dc, dc in each dc across to last dc before next ch-2 sp, 2 dc in next dc, dc in next ch-2 sp, ch 2**; skip 3-dc dec, 2 dc in next dc, dc in next dc, 2 dc in next dc, skip 3-dc dec; rep from * to ** once; dc in last 2 dc: 259 dc and 4 ch-2 sps; ch 3, turn.

Row 35: Dc in next dc; *ch 2, dc in next ch-2 sp, 2 dc in next dc, dc in each dc across to last dc before next ch-2 sp, 2 dc in next dc, dc in next ch-2 sp, ch 2**; dc in next dc, 2-dc dec over next 3 sts, dc in next dc; rep from * to ** once; dc in last 2 dc: 265 dc and 4 ch-2 sps; ch 3, turn.

Row 36: Dc in next dc; *ch 2, dc in next ch-2 sp, 2 dc in next dc, dc in each dc across to last dc before next ch-2 sp, 2 dc in next dc, dc in next ch-2 sp, ch 2**; 3-dc dec; rep from * to ** once; dc in last 2 dc: 263 dc and 4 ch-2 sps; ch 3, turn.

EDGING

Row 1: Dc in next dc, ch 2, skip first ch-2 sp; *dc in next dc, ch 1, skip next dc**; rep from * to ** across to last dc before next ch-2 sp; dc in next dc, ch 1, skip next ch-2 sp, dc in next dc, ch 1, skip next dc; rep from * to ** across to last dc before next ch-2 sp; dc in next dc, ch 2, skip last ch-2 sp, dc in last 2 dc: 139 dc, 2 ch-2 sps and 134 ch-1 sps; ch 3, turn.

Row 2: Dc in next dc, ch 2, skip first ch-2 sp, V-st in next dc; *skip next ch-1 sp, V-st in next dc**; rep from * to ** across to last ch-2 sp; ch 2, skip last ch-2 sp, dc in last 2 dc: 135 V-sts, 4 dc and 2 ch-2 sps; ch 3, turn.

Row 3: Dc in next dc, ch 2, skip first ch-2 sp; *shell in ch-2 sp of next V-st**; rep from * to ** across to last ch-2 sp; ch 2, skip last ch-2 sp, dc in last 2 dc: 135 shells, 4 dc and 2 ch-2 sps; ch 3, turn.

Row 4: Dc in next dc, ch 2, skip first ch-2 sp; *lg shell in ch-2 sp of next shell**; rep from * to ** across to last ch-2 sp; ch 2, skip last ch-2 sp, dc in last 2 dc: 135 lg shells, 4 dc and 2 ch-2 sps. Finish off; weave in ends.

QUICK AND COLORFUL

Brighten the heart of the recipient with this cheerful wrap. Its easy pattern will fly off your hook.

Skill Level: Easy ■■□□

DESIGNED BY JEAN LEINHAUSER

Size

Approximately 20½" wide x 67" long
(52 cm x 170 cm)

Materials

Worsted weight yarn 【4】
[53% wool, 47% acrylic, 1.75 ounces, 147 yards
(50 grams, 135 meters) per skein]
        6 skeins variegated

Note: *Photographed model made with Lion Brand®
Amazing® #212 Mauna Loa.*

Size J (6 mm) crochet hook (or size required for
gauge)

Gauge

10 dc and 5 dc rows = 4" (10 cm)

Stitch Guide

Small shell: Work (2 dc, ch 2, 2 dc) in specified st or sp.

Medium shell: Work (3 dc, ch 3, 3 dc) in
specified st or sp.

Large shell: Work (4 dc, ch 4, 4 dc) in specified st or sp.

Note: *When working in shells, work in ch-sp of
each shell. When instructions specify to skip a
certain number of dc, do not count dc of shells.
Only count dc in 5-dc sections between shells.*

INSTRUCTIONS

Ch 56.

Row 1 (right side): Sc in 2nd ch from hook
and in each rem ch across: 55 sc; ch 3 (counts
as dc on next row now and throughout), turn.

Row 2: Dc in next 4 sc, (skip next 2 sc, small
shell in next sc, skip next 2 sc, dc in next 5 sc)
5 times: 5 small shells and 30 dc (six 5-dc sections); ch 3, turn.

Rows 3-77: Dc in next 4 dc, (small shell in
next small shell, dc in next 5 dc) 5 times,
working last dc on last rep in 3rd ch of beg
ch-3; ch 3, turn. At end of last row, do not finish off.

FIRST EDGING

Row 1 (right side): Skip next dc of first 5-dc
section, medium shell in next dc, (skip next 2
dc of same 5-dc section, medium shell in next
small shell, skip first 2 dc of next 5-dc section,
medium shell in next dc) 5 times, skip next dc
of same 5-dc section, dc in 3rd ch of beg ch-3:
11 medium shells and 2 dc; ch 3, turn.

Row 2: Large shell in next medium shell, (dc
in sp between shells, large shell in next medium shell) 10 times, dc in 3rd ch of beg ch-3:
11 large shells and 2 dc; ch 3, turn.

Row 3: Large shell in next large shell, (dc in dc
between shells, large shell in next large shell)
10 times, dc in 3rd ch of beg ch-3. Finish off;
weave in ends.

SECOND EDGING

Row 1: With right side facing and piece held
with foundation ch at top, join with sl st in
free lps of ch at base of last sc worked on Row
1, working in free lps of foundation ch, skip
next ch, medium shell in next ch, (skip next
4 chs, medium shell in next ch) 10 times, skip
next ch, dc in last ch: 11 medium shells and 2
dc; ch 3, turn.

Note: *Medium shells should line up with base of
small shells and middle dc of each 5-dc section.*

Rows 2 and 3: Rep Rows 2 and 3 on First Edging. Finish off; weave in ends.

CROSSES AND DIAMONDS

Ten full squares and four half squares made with crosses and diamonds motifs are joined in one glorious shawl!

Skill Level: Easy ▭▭▭▭▭

DESIGNED BY JULEE A. REEVES

Size

Approximately 72" wide x 36" long at center back point (183 cm x 91 cm)

Materials

Worsted weight yarn
[100% acrylic, 5 ounces, 256 yards (140 grams, 234 meters) per skein]

    7 skeins tan (A)
    1 skein off-white (B)

Note: *Photographed model made with Red Heart® Soft Yarn® # 9114 Honey (A) and #4601 Off-White (B)*

Size G (4 mm) crochet hook (or size required for gauge)

Gauge

Rnds 1 and 2 of full motif = 2¼" (6.5 cm) square
Full motif = 12" (30 cm) square

Stitch Guide

Reverse single crochet (rev sc): Working from left to right, insert hook in next st to right of last st and draw up a lp, YO and draw through 2 lps on hook: rev sc made.

To join with sc: Make a slip knot and place on hook, insert hook in specified st and draw up a lp, YO and draw through 2 lps on hook.

Note: *When working into chains in "cross" section of full motifs and half motifs, work into front and back loops of each chain.*

INSTRUCTIONS

FULL MOTIF (MAKE 10)

With Color A, ch 3; join with sl st in first ch to form a ring.

Rnd 1 (right side): Ch 5 (counts as first dc and ch-2 sp), (3 dc in ring, ch 2) 3 times, 2 dc in ring: 12 dc and 4 corner ch-2 sps; join with sl st in 3rd ch of beg ch-5.

Rnd 2: Ch 3 (counts as first dc here and throughout); *(2 dc, ch 2, 2 dc) in corner ch-2 sp**; dc in next 3 dc; rep from * around, ending last rep at **; dc in last 2 dc: 28 dc and 4 corner ch-2 sps; join with sl st in 3rd ch of beg ch-3.

Rnd 3: Sl st in next dc, ch 3; *dc in next dc, (2 dc, ch 2, 2 dc) in corner ch-2 sp, dc in next 3 dc, ch 1, skip next dc, dc in next 3 dc, (2 dc, ch 2, 2 dc) in corner ch-2 sp, dc in next

instructions continued on page 16

2 dc**; (ch 1, skip next dc, dc in next dc) 2 times; rep from * to ** once; ch 1, skip next dc, dc in next dc, ch 1, skip next dc: 36 dc, 4 corner ch-2 sps and 6 chs; join as before.

Rnd 4: Ch 3; *dc in next 3 dc, (2 dc, ch 2, 2 dc) in corner ch-2 sp, dc in next 4 dc, ch 1, skip next dc, dc in next ch, ch 1, skip next dc, dc in next 4 dc, (2 dc, ch 2, 2 dc) in corner ch-2 sp, dc in next 4 dc**; (ch 1, skip next ch, dc in next dc) 2 times; rep from * to ** once; ch 1, skip next ch, dc in next dc, ch 1, skip next ch: 52 dc, 4 corner ch-2 sps and 8 chs; join.

Rnd 5: Ch 3; *dc in next 5 dc, (2 dc, ch 2, 2 dc) in corner ch-2 sp, dc in next 5 dc, (ch 1, skip next dc, dc in next ch) 2 times, ch 1, skip next dc, dc in next 5 dc, (2 dc, ch 2, 2 dc) in corner ch-2 sp, dc in next 6 dc**; (ch 1, skip next ch, dc in next dc) 2 times; rep from * to ** once; ch 1, skip next ch, dc in next dc, ch 1, skip next ch: 66 dc, 4 corner ch-2 sps and 10 chs; join.

Rnd 6: Ch 3; *dc in next 7 dc, (2 dc, ch 2, 2 dc) in corner ch-2 sp, dc in next 6 dc, (ch 1, skip next dc, dc in next ch) 3 times, ch 1, skip next dc, dc in next 6 dc, (2 dc, ch 2, 2 dc) in corner ch-2 sp, dc in next 8 dc**; (ch 1, skip next ch, dc in next dc) 2 times; rep from * to ** once; ch 1, skip next ch, dc in next dc, ch 1, skip next ch: 80 dc, 4 corner ch-2 sps and 12 chs; join.

Rnd 7: Ch 4 (counts as first dc and ch), skip next dc, dc in next dc, ch 1, skip next dc, dc in next 6 dc; *(2 dc, ch 2, 2 dc) in corner ch-2 sp, dc in next 8 dc, dc in next ch, (ch 1, skip next dc, dc in next ch) 3 times, dc in next 8 dc, (2 dc, ch 2, 2 dc) in corner ch-2 sp, dc in next 6 dc, (ch 1, skip next dc, dc in next dc) 2 times**; (ch 1, skip next ch, dc in next dc) 2 times, (ch 1, skip next dc, dc in next dc) 2 times, dc in next 5 dc; rep from * to ** once;

ch 1, skip next ch, dc in next dc, ch 1, skip next ch: 90 dc, 4 corner ch-2 sps and 18 chs; join with sl st in 3rd ch of beg ch-4.

Rnd 8: Ch 3; *(dc in next ch, dc in next dc) 2 times, dc in next 7 dc, (2 dc, ch 2, 2 dc) in corner ch-2 sp, dc in next 11 dc, dc in next ch, (ch 1, skip next dc, dc in next ch) 2 times, dc in next 11 dc, (2 dc, ch 2, 2 dc) in corner ch-2 sp, dc in next 8 dc, (dc in next ch, dc in next dc) 2 times**; (ch 1, skip next ch, dc in next dc) 2 times; rep from * to ** once; ch 1, skip next ch, dc in next dc, ch 1, skip next ch: 116 dc, 4 corner ch-2 sps and 8 chs; join with sl st in 3rd ch of beg ch-3.

Rnd 9: Ch 3; *dc in next 13 dc, (2 dc, ch 2, 2 dc) in corner ch-2 sp, dc in next 14 dc, dc in next ch, ch 1, skip next dc, dc in next ch, dc in next 14 dc, (2 dc, ch 2, 2 dc) in corner ch-2 sp, dc in next 14 dc**; (ch 1, skip next

ch, dc in next dc) 2 times; rep from * to ** once; ch 1, skip next ch, dc in next dc, ch 1, skip next ch: 134 dc, 4 corner ch-2 sps and 6 chs; join.

Rnd 10: Ch 3; *dc in next 15 dc, (2 dc, ch 2, 2 dc) in corner ch-2 sp, dc in next 17 dc, dc in next ch, dc in next 17 dc, (2 dc, ch 2, 2 dc) in corner ch-2 sp, dc in next 16 dc**; (dc in next ch, dc in next dc) 2 times; rep from * to ** once; dc in next ch, dc in next dc, dc in next ch: 156 dc and 4 corner ch-2 sps; join.

Rnd 11: Ch 4 (counts as dc and ch), skip next dc, dc in next dc, (ch 1, skip next dc, dc in next dc) 7 times, ch 1, skip next dc, (2 dc, ch 2, 2 dc) in corner ch-2 sp; *(ch 1, skip next dc, dc in next dc) 19 times, ch 1, skip next dc, (2 dc, ch 2, 2 dc) in corner ch-2 sp; rep from * 2 times more; (ch 1, skip next dc, dc in next dc) 10 times, ch 1, skip next dc: 92 dc, 4 corner ch-2 sps and 80 chs; join with sl st in 3rd ch of beg ch-4.

Rnd 12: Ch 2 (counts as first hdc); *hdc in BL of each ch and dc across to corner ch-2 sp, 2 hdc in BL of first ch in corner, ch 2, 2 hdc in BL of 2nd ch in corner; rep from * 3 times more; hdc in BL of each rem ch and dc: 188 hdc and 4 corner ch-2 sps; join with sl st in 2nd ch of beg ch-2, changing to Color B. Drop Color A to wrong side.

Rnd 13: With Color B, ch 1; *sc in BL of same ch as joining, sc in BL of each hdc across to corner ch-2 sp, sc in BL of first ch in corner, ch 2, sc in BL of 2nd ch in corner; rep from * 3 times more; sc in BL of each rem hdc: 196 sc and 4 corner ch-2 sps; join with sl st in first sc, changing to Color A. Finish off Color B.

Rnd 14: With Color A, ch 1; *sc in BL of same sc as joining, sc in BL of each sc across to corner ch-2 sp, sc in BL of first ch in corner, ch 2, sc in BL of 2nd ch in corner; rep from * 3 times more; sc in BL of each rem sc: 204 sc and 4 corner ch-2 sps; join with sl st in first sc. Finish Off Color A. Weave in all ends.

HALF MOTIF (make 4)

Row 1 (right side): With Color A, ch 4, (3 dc, ch 2, 4 dc) in 4th ch from hook (3 skipped chs count as a dc): 8 dc and 1 corner ch-2 sp; loosely ch 3 (counts as dc on following row here and throughout), turn.

Row 2: Work 2 dc in first dc, dc in next 3 dc, (2 dc, ch 2, 2 dc) in corner ch-2 sp, dc in next 3 dc, 3 dc in 4th ch of beg ch-4: 16 dc and 1 corner ch-2 sp; loosely ch 3, turn.

Row 3: Work 2 dc in first dc, dc in next 2 dc, (ch 1, skip next dc, dc in next dc) 2 times, dc in next dc, (2 dc, ch 2, 2 dc) in corner ch-2 sp, dc in next 3 dc, ch 1, skip next dc, dc in next 3 dc, 3 dc in 3rd ch of beg ch-3: 21 dc, 1 corner ch-2 sp and 3 chs; loosely ch 3, turn.

Row 4: Work 2 dc in first dc, dc in next 4 dc, ch 1, skip next dc, dc in next ch, ch 1, skip next dc, dc in next 4 dc, (2 dc, ch 2, 2 dc) in corner ch-2 sp, dc in next 4 dc, (ch 1, skip next ch, dc in next dc) 2 times, dc in next 3 dc, 3 dc in 3rd ch of beg ch-3: 28 dc, 1 corner ch-2 sp and 4 chs; loosely ch 3, turn.

Row 5: Work 2 dc in first dc, dc in next 6 dc, (ch 1, skip next ch, dc in next dc) 2 times, dc in next 5 dc, (2 dc, ch 2, 2 dc) in corner ch-2 sp, dc in next 5 dc, (ch 1, skip next dc, dc in next ch) 2 times, ch 1, skip next dc, dc in next 5 dc, 3 dc in 3rd ch of beg ch-3: 35 dc, 1 corner ch-2 sp and 5 chs; loosely ch 3, turn.

Row 6: Work 2 dc in first dc, dc in next 6 dc, (ch 1, skip next dc, dc in next ch) 3 times, ch 1, skip next dc, dc in next 6 dc, (2 dc, ch 2, 2 dc) in corner ch-2 sp, dc in next 8 dc, (ch 1, skip next ch, dc in next dc) 2 times, dc in next 7 dc, 3 dc in 3rd ch of beg ch-3: 42 dc, 1 corner ch-2 sp and 6 chs; loosely ch 3, turn.

Row 7: Work 2 dc in first dc, dc in next 6 dc, (ch 1, skip next dc, dc in next dc) 2 times, (ch 1, skip next ch, dc in next dc) 2 times, (ch 1, skip next dc, dc in next dc) 2 times, dc

instructions continued on page 18

in next 5 dc, (2 dc, ch 2, 2 dc) in corner ch-2 sp, dc in next 8 dc, dc in next ch, (ch 1, skip next dc, dc in next ch) 3 times, dc in next 8 dc, 3 dc in 3rd ch beg ch-3: 47 dc, 1 corner ch-2 sp and 9 chs; loosely ch 3, turn.

Row 8: Work 2 dc in first dc, dc in next 11 dc, dc in next ch, (ch 1, skip next dc, dc in next ch) 2 times, dc in next 11 dc, (2 dc, ch 2, 2 dc) in corner ch-2 sp, dc in next 8 dc, (dc in next ch, dc in next dc) 2 times, (ch 1, skip next ch, dc in next dc) 2 times, (dc in next ch, dc in next dc) 2 times, dc in next 7 dc, 3 dc in 3rd ch of beg ch-3: 60 dc, 1 corner ch-2 sp and 4 chs; loosely ch 3, turn.

Row 9: Work 2 dc in first dc, dc in next 14 dc, (ch 1, skip next ch, dc in next dc) 2 times, dc in next 13 dc, (2 dc, ch 2, 2 dc) in corner ch-2 sp, dc in next 14 dc, dc in next ch, ch 1, skip next dc, dc in next ch, dc in next 14 dc, 3 dc in 3rd ch of beg ch-3: 69 dc, 1 corner ch-2 sp and 3 chs; loosely ch 3, turn.

Row 10: Work 2 dc in first dc, dc in next 17 dc, dc in next ch, dc in next 17 dc, (2 dc, ch 2, 2 dc) in corner ch-2 sp, dc in next 16 dc, (dc in next ch, dc in next dc) 2 times, dc in next 15 dc, 3 dc in 3rd ch of beg ch-3: 80 dc and 1 corner ch-2 sp; loosely ch 3, turn.

Row 11: Work 2 dc in first dc; *(ch 1, skip next dc, dc in next dc) 19 times, ch 1, skip next dc**; (2 dc, ch 2, 2 dc) in corner ch-2 sp; rep from * to ** once; 3 dc in 3rd ch of beg ch-3: 48 dc, 1 corner ch-2 sp and 40 chs; loosely ch 2 (counts as hdc on following row), turn.

Row 12: Work 2 hdc in FL of first dc, hdc in FL of each dc and ch across to corner ch-2 sp, 2 hdc in FL of first ch in corner, ch 2, 2 hdc in FL of 2nd ch in corner, hdc in FL of each dc and ch across to last dc, 3 hdc in FL of 3rd ch of beg ch-3, changing to Color B in last hdc: 96 hdc and 1 corner ch-2 sp; with Color B, loosely ch 1, turn. Drop Color A to wrong side.

Row 13: With Color B, 2 sc in BL of first Hdc, sc in BL of each hdc across to corner ch-2 sp, sc in BL of first ch in corner, ch 2, sc in BL of 2nd ch in corner, sc in BL of each hdc across to beg ch-2, 2 sc in BL of 2nd ch of beg ch-2: 100 sc and 1 corner ch-2 sp. Do not turn. Finish off Color B.

Row 14: With right side still facing, place Color A back on hook, ch 1, 2 sc in BL of first sc, sc in BL of each sc across to corner ch-2 sp, sc in BL of first ch in corner, ch 2, sc in BL of 2nd ch in corner, sc in BL of each sc across to last sc, 2 sc in BL of last sc: 104 sc and 1 corner ch-2 sp. Finish off Color A. Weave in all ends.

Assembly

With right sides together, referring to Assembly Diagram, join full motifs and half motifs together with whip stitch in BL only.

Edging

With right side facing, join Color A with sc in corner ch-2 sp at bottom tip of shawl, work rev sc evenly spaced around entire outer edge of shawl, working sc in BL of every other sc on edges of full motifs and 1-2 sc in each row on diagonal edges of half motifs; join with sl st in first sc. Fasten off. Weave in ends.

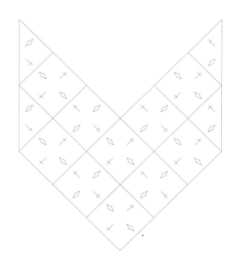

Bottom Tip

THE PRIMROSE WRAP

Make it fast and make it beautiful! Quick to make and lovely to look at: the perfect prayer shawl.

Skill Level: Intermediate ⬛⬛⬛⬜

DESIGNED BY MARGARET HUBERT

Size

Approximately 18" long x 58" wide
(46 cm x 147 cm)

Materials

Worsted weight yarn (4)
[100% acrylic, 6 ounces, 315 yards (170 grams,
288 meters) per skein]
    2 skeins lavender

Note: *Photographed model made with Caron® Simply Soft® #9756 Lavender Blue*
Size K (6.5 mm) crochet hook (or size required for gauge)
Stitch markers

Gauge

7 dc and 6 ch-2 sps = 6" (15 cm)
6 mesh rows = 4" (10 cm)

Stitch Guide

Cluster (CL): *YO twice, insert hook in specified st and draw up a lp, (YO and draw through 2 lps on hook) twice; rep from * once more; YO and draw through all 3 lps on hook: CL made.

Triple treble crochet (trtr): YO 4 times, insert hook in specified st and draw up a lp, [YO and draw through 2 lps on hook] 5 times: trtr made.

INSTRUCTIONS

Ch 203 loosely.

Row 1 (right side): Dc in 8th ch from hook (skipped chs count as dc and ch-2 sp); *ch 2, sk next 2 chs, dc in next ch; rep from * across: 66 ch-2 sps; ch 5 (counts as dc and ch-2 sp on next row throughout), turn.

Row 2: *Dc in next dc, ch 2; rep from * across to turning ch; sk next 2 chs, dc in next ch; ch 5, turn.

Row 3: Rep Row 2, ending with ch 1, turn, instead of ch 5, turn.

instructions continued on page 21

Row 4: Sc in first dc; *ch 9, sk next dc, work (sc, ch 4, CL) in next dc, sk next dc, work (CL, ch 4, sc) in next dc; rep from * 15 times more; ch 9, sk next dc, sc in 3rd ch of turning ch-5: 32 CL and 17 ch-9 lps; ch 10 (counts as trtr and ch 4 on next row), turn.

Row 5: Sc in first ch-9 lp; *ch 4, in next CL work (CL, ch 4, sl st, ch 4, CL); ch 4, skip next CL, sc in next ch-9 lp; rep from * 15 times more; ch 4, trtr in last sc: 32 CL and 34 ch-4 sps; ch 1, turn.

Row 6: Sc in first trtr; *ch 5, sc in next CL; rep from * across to turning ch; ch 5, sc in 6th ch of turning ch-10: 33 ch-5 sps; ch 5, turn.

Row 7: Dc in first ch-5 sp, ch 2, dc in next sc; *ch 2, dc in next ch-5 sp, ch 2, dc in next sc; rep from * across: 66 ch-2 sps, ch 5, turn.

Rows 8 through 27: Rep Rows 2 through 7 three times more, then rep Rows 2 and 3 once more. At end of Row 27, finish off.

EDGING

Place 15 markers evenly spaced across one short edge of wrap, including corners, placing markers in top of stitches instead of in chain spaces as much as possible. With right side facing and short edge of wrap at top, join with sl st in marked right-hand corner st, 7 tr in next marked st; *sc in next marked st, 7 tr in next marked st; rep from * 5 times more; sc in marked left-hand corner st: 7 shells. Finish off.

Repeat edging on other short edge of wrap.

BLOCKING

Lay wrap flat on a padded surface. Sprinkle with water, pat into shape and allow to dry.

21

A HEART IN HER POCKET

Every little girl will certainly be delighted with all of the warmth provided by this adorable shawl with its pockets made out of hearts.

Skill Level: Intermediate

DESIGNED BY TAMMY HILDEBRAND

Note: *Instructions are written for size 6; changes for larger sizes 8, 10 and 12 are in parentheses.*

Sizes

	6	8	10	12
Width	26¾"	28¾"	30¾"	32¾"
Length (front to back)	36¼"	37½"	38¾"	40¼"

Materials

Worsted weight yarn
[97% acrylic, 3% metallic polyester, 3.5 ounces, 280 yards (100 grams, 256 meters) per skein]

    3 skeins white (A)

    1 skein pink (B)

Note: *Photographed model made with Red Heart® Shimmer™, #1010 Snow (A) and #1715 Hot Pink (B)*

Size I (5.5mm) crochet hook (or size required for gauge)

Gauge

12 esc and 12 rows in pattern = 4" (10 cm)

Stitch Guide

Extended Single Crochet (esc): Insert hook in specified st and draw up a lp, YO and draw through first lp on hook, YO and draw through both lps on hook: esc made.

Single crochet decrease (sc dec): Insert hook in next st or sp and draw up a lp, insert hook in 2nd st or sp, pull up lp, yo and pull through all 3 lps on hook.

Note: *Shawl is worked from side-to-side, beginning by working right front and back at same time, then working on back stitches only to form back of neck before adding new stitches to complete the left side of shawl. Pockets and edging are added afterward.*

INSTRUCTIONS

RIGHT FRONT AND BACK

With A, ch 108 (112, 116, 120).

Row 1 (right side): Sc in 2nd ch from hook and in each rem ch across: 107 (111, 115, 119) sc; ch 1, turn.

Row 2: Esc in first st; *ch 1, skip next st, esc in next st; rep from * across: 54 (56, 58, 60) esc and 53 (55, 57, 59) ch-1 sps; ch 1, turn.

Row 3: Sc in each st and ch-1 sp across: 107 (111, 115, 119) sc; ch 1, turn.

Rows 4 through 33 (35, 37, 39): Rep Rows 2 and 3, 15 (16, 17, 18) times more.

CENTER BACK

Row 1 (wrong side): Esc in first st; *ch 1, skip next st, esc in next st; rep from * 25 (26, 27, 28) times more: 26 (27, 28, 29) esc and 25 (26, 27, 28) ch-1 sps; ch 1, turn, leaving rem sts unworked.

Row 2: Sc in each st and ch-1 sp across: 51 (53, 55, 57) sc; ch 1, turn.

Row 3: Esc in first st; *ch 1, skip next st, esc in next st; rep from * across: 26 (27, 28, 29) esc and 25 (26, 27, 28) ch-1 sps; ch 1, turn.

Rows 4 through 12 (14, 16, 18): Rep Rows 2 and 3, 4 (5, 6, 7) more times, then rep Row 2 once more.

LEFT FRONT AND BACK

instructions continued on page 24

LEFT FRONT AND BACK

Row 1 (wrong side): Esc in first st; *ch 1, skip next st, esc in next st; rep from * across, ch 57 (59, 61, 63), turn: 26 (27, 28, 29) esc, 25 (26, 27, 28) ch-1 sps, and 57 (59, 61, 63) chs.

Row 2: Sc in 2nd ch from hook, sc in each rem ch, then continuing on back, sc in each st and ch-1 sp across: 107 (111, 115, 119) sc; ch 1, turn.

Rows 3 through 34 (36, 38, 40): Rep Rows 2 and 3 on Right Front and Back, 16 (17, 18, 19) times more. At end of last row, finish off.

EDGING

Rnd 1: With right side facing, join B with sc in first st on Row 34 of Left Front, ch 3, sc in same st as joining; working around entire outer edge of shawl, ch 2, skip next st or row; *sc in next st or row, ch 2, skip next st or row**; rep from * to ** across to next outer corner***; (sc, ch 3, sc) in next outer corner; ch 2, skip next st or row; rep from * around, ending last rep at ***; join with sl st in beg-sc. Do not work (sc, ch 3, sc) at inner neck corners. Do not turn.

Rnd 2: Sl st in next ch-2 sp, ch 2 (counts as hdc), 2 hdc in same ch-2 sp, sl st around post of next sc; *3 hdc in next ch-2 sp, sl st around post of next sc; rep from * around; join with sl st 2nd ch of beg ch-2. Finish off; weave in ends.

Heart Pocket (make 2)

Row 1 (right side): Starting at bottom of heart with B, ch 2, sc in 2nd ch from hook: 1 sc; ch 1, turn.

Row 2: Work 3 sc in sc: 3 sc; ch 1, turn.

Row 3: Sc in each st across; ch 1, turn.

Row 4: Work 2 sc in first st, sc in each st across to last st, 2 sc in last st: 5 sc; ch 1, turn.

Rows 5 through 10: Rep Rows 3 and 4 three times: 11 sc at end of Row 10.

Rows 11 through 14: Rep Row 4 four times: 19 sc at end of Row 14.

Rows 15 and 16: Rep Row 3 twice.

Row 17: Work (sc dec) twice, sc in next 11 sts, (sc dec) twice: 15 sc; ch 1, turn.

Row 18: Sc in first st, hdc in next st, 3 dc in next st, hdc in next st, sc in next 2 sts, ch 1, skip next st, sl st in next st, ch 1, skip next st, sc in next 2 sts, hdc in next st, 3 dc in next st, hdc in next st, sc in last st: 17 sts (including sl st); ch 1, turn.

Row 19: Skip first st, sc in next st, hdc in next st, 3 dc in next st, hdc in next st, sc dec, ch 1, skip next ch, sl st in same st on Row 17 as sl st worked on Row 18, ch 1, skip next ch, sc dec, hdc in next st, 3 dc in next st, hdc in next st, sc in next st, skip last st: 15 sts (including sl st). Do not turn.

Edging

Rnd 1 (right side): Ch 1, pivot piece to work in edges of rows on left edge of heart, 3 sc in first row (last sc worked on Row 19), sc in each row down to bottom point, 3 sc in free lp of ch at bottom point, sc in each row up to last row, 3 sc in last row; working in sts across Row 19, skip first st, sc in next 6 sts, ch 1, sl st in same st on Row 17 as sl st worked on Rows 18 and 19, ch 1, sc in next 6 sts; join with sl st in first sc.

Rnd 2: *Ch 3, sl st in next st**; rep from * to ** around to top center sl st, ch 1, sl st in same st on Row 17 as sl st worked on Rows 18 and 19, ch 1, sl st in next st; rep from * to ** across to beg; ch 3; join with sl st in first sl st. Finish off, leaving a long tail for sewing.

With right side of shawl and right side of hearts facing, using yarn needle, using photo for placement, stitch 2 side edges of one heart to each side of front, sewing through Rnd 1 of edging and leaving top open for pocket.

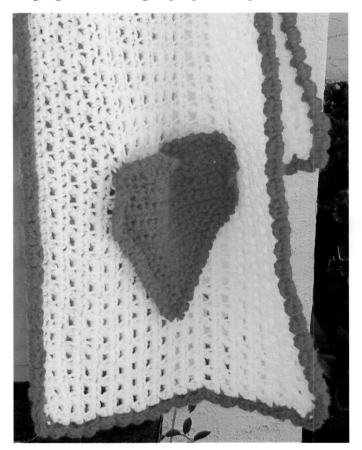

LOVELY LACE

The perfect wrap for a warm summer evening!

Skill Level: Easy

DESIGNED BY JEAN LEINHAUSER

Size

Approximately 18" x 56"

Materials

Worsted weight yarn [4]
  [100% acrylic, 3.5 ounces, 190 yards, (100 grams, 174 meters) per skein]
    2 skeins blue
    2 skeins off-white

Note: *Photographed model made with Red Heart® Classic® #0627 light periwinkle and #0003 off white*

Size J/10 (6 mm) crochet hook or size required for gauge

Gauge

3 sts = 1"

INSTRUCTIONS

With blue, ch 140.

Row 1 (right side): Work 2 dc in 4th ch from hook (beg 3 skipped chs count as a dc), *skip next 3 chs, (3 dc, ch 3, 3 dc) in next ch (shell made), sk next 3 chs, 3 dc in next ch, rep from * across, turn.

Row 2: Sl st in first 2 sts, ch 3 (counts as a dc on this and following rows), 2 dc in same st, *shell in ch-3 sp of next shell, 3 dc in 2nd dc of next 3-dc group, rep from * across, changing to white in last dc, finish off blue. Turn.

Row 3: Sl st in first 2 sts, ch 3, 2 dc in same st, *shell in ch-3 sp of next shell, 3 dc in 2nd dc of next 3-dc group, rep from * across, turn.

Row 4: Sl st in first 2 sts, ch 3, 2 dc in same st, *shell in ch-3 sp of next shell, 3 dc in 2nd dc of next 3-dc group, rep from * across, changing to blue in last dc, finish off white. Turn.

Row 5: Sl st in first 2 sts, ch 3, 2 dc in same st, *shell in ch-3 sp of next shell, 3 dc in 2nd dc of next 3-dc group, rep from * across, turn.

Row 6: Sl st in first 2 sts, ch 3, 2 dc in same st, *shell in ch-3 sp of next shell, 3 dc in 2nd dc of next 3-dc group, rep from * across, changing to white in last dc, finish off blue. Turn.

Rows 7 - 18: Rep Rows 3-6 three times. Finish off; weave in ends.

TOP EDGING

Row 1: Hold piece with Right Side facing and beg ch at top, join blue with sc in first ch, working in unused lps of chs and in rem chs of beg ch, sc evenly spaced across. Do not turn.

Row 2: Ch 1, working left to right, work reverse sc in each sc across.

Finish off; weave in ends.

EDGED WITH CROSSES

The perfect border for a prayer shawl: a row of large and small crosses. Simple yet elegant.

Skill Level: Easy ◼◼◻◻

DESIGNED BY MARY JANE HALL

Size

Approximately 21" long x 55" wide
(53 cm x 140 cm), plus cross motifs

Materials

Worsted weight yarn

[100% acrylic, 6 ounces, 315 yards (170 grams,
  288 meters) per skein]

    1 skein black (A)

    1 skein red (B)

Note: *Photographed model made with Caron® Simply Soft® #9727 Black (A) and #9730 Autumn Red (B)*

Sizes N (9.0 mm) and F (3.75 mm) crochet hooks
(or sizes required for gauge)

Gauge

With N hook, shell = 2" (5 cm) wide;
1 pattern rep = 5" (13 cm) wide; 3 rows in pattern =
2$\frac{1}{2}$" (6 cm) long
With F hook, Large Cross Motif = 4$\frac{1}{2}$" x 3$\frac{3}{4}$"
(11 cm x 10 cm)
With F hook, Small Cross Motif = 3$\frac{1}{2}$" x 2$\frac{3}{4}$"
(9 cm x 7 cm)

Stitch Guide

Shell: Work 5 dc in specified st or sp.

Notes: *To make shawl wider, add more chs to foundation ch in multiples of 12 chs and make more large and/or small cross motifs. To make shawl longer, work more multiples of Rows 2-4. Keep in mind that because of the loose stitches, the finished shawl will stretch, therefore making it longer.*

INSTRUCTIONS

Starting at top with N hook and A, ch 137.

Row 1 (right side): Sc in 7th ch from hook (skipped chs count as dc and ch-2 sp); *ch 2, skip next 3 chs, shell in next ch, ch 2, skip next 3 chs, sc in next ch**; ch 5, skip next 3 chs, sc in next ch; rep from * across, ending last rep at **; ch 2, skip next ch, dc in last ch: 11 shells, 2 dc, 22 sc, 10 ch-5 sps and 24 ch-2 sps; ch 1, turn.

Row 2: Sc in first dc; *ch 2, (dc in next dc, ch 1) 4 times, dc in next dc, ch 2**; skip next ch-2 sp, sc in center ch of next ch-5 sp; rep from * across, ending last rep at **; skip next 2 chs and sc; sc over beg ch-5 of Row 1: 55 dc and 22 ch-2 sps; ch 3 (counts as dc on following row), turn.

Row 3: *(Dc in next dc, ch 2) 4 times, dc in next dc; rep from * across; dc in last sc: 57 dc and 44 ch-2 sps; ch 5 (counts as dc and ch-2 sp on following row), turn.

Row 4: *Sc in next ch-2 sp, ch 2, skip next dc, shell in next dc, ch 2, skip next ch-2 sp, sc in next ch-2 sp**; ch 5; rep from * across, ending last rep at **; ch 2, dc in 3rd ch of turning ch-3: 11 shells, 2 dc, 22 sc, 10 ch-5 sps and 24 ch-2 sps; ch 1, turn.

Rows 5-24: Rep Rows 2-4, 6 times more, then rep Rows 2 and 3 once more. At end of last row, ch 1 (instead of 5), turn.

instructions continued on page 30

EDGING

Work 3 sc in first st, sc evenly around edge of shawl, working 3 sc in each corner; join with sl st in first sc. Finish off; weave in ends.

Large Cross Motif (make 6)

With F hook and B, ch 6; join with sl st to form a ring.

Rnd 1: Ch 1, 16 sc in ring: 16 sc; join with sl st in first sc.

Rnd 2: Ch 1, sc in same st as joining, sc in next sc; *(sc, ch 9, sc) in next sc, sc in next 3 sc; rep from * 2 times more, (sc, ch 16, sc) in next sc, sc in last sc: 20 sc, 1 ch-16 lp and 3 ch-9 lps; join with sl st in first sc.

Rnd 3: Ch 1, sc in same st as joining, sl st in next sc; *skip next sc, work (2 hdc, 17 dc, 2 hdc) in next ch-9 lp, skip next 2 sc, sl st in next sc; rep from * 2 times more, skip next sc, work (2 hdc, 25 dc, 2 hdc) in next ch-16 lp, skip last 2 sc: 76 dc, 16 hdc, 4 sc and 4 sl sts; join with sl st in first sc. Finish off, leaving a 12" (30 cm) tail.

Small Cross Motif (make 5)

With F hook and B, ch 5; join with sl st to form a ring.

Rnd 1: Ch 1, 12 sc in ring; join with sl st in first sc: 12 sc.

Rnd 2: Ch 1, sc in same st as joining, sc in next sc; *(sc, ch 6, sc) in next sc, sc in next 2 sc; rep from * 2 times more, (sc, ch 13, sc) in next sc: 16 sc, 1 ch-13 lp and 3 ch-6 lps; join with sl st in first sc.

Rnd 3: Ch 1, sc in same st as joining, sl st in next sc; *work (2 hdc, 8 dc, 2 hdc) in next ch-6 lp, skip next sc, sl st in next sc; rep from * 2 times more, work (2 hdc, 16 dc, 2 hdc) in next ch-13 lp; join with sl st in first sc: 40 dc, 16 hdc, 4 sc and 4 sl sts. Finish off, leaving a 12" (30cm) tail.

FINISHING

With 12" (30 cm) tail, sew inside edge at base of each ch-lp on shells together. With right side of shawl and crosses facing, sew top of crosses to bottom edge of shawl at center of each shell, alternating large and small crosses, as shown in photograph. Weave in all ends.

BRIGHT SHELLS

Rows of colorful shells make this a glorious shawl. Choose a multi-colored yarn, and the yarn will make the project beautiful!

Skill Level: Intermediate ◨◼◼◻

DESIGNED BY TAMMY HILDEBRAND

Size

Approximately 19" long x 64" wide along neck edge between points (48 cm x 163 cm)

Materials

Worsted weight yarn
[100% acrylic, 3.5 ounces, 209 yards (100 grams, 191 meters) per skein]
    4 skeins multi-colored

Note: *Photographed model made with Bernat® Mosaic #44203 Aura.*

Size J (6.0 mm) crochet hook (or size required for gauge)

Gauge

2 shells and 2 sc in pattern = 4" (10 cm)
6 rows in pattern = 4" (10 cm)

Stitch Guide

Shell: Work 5 dc in specified st or sp: shell made.

Beginning V-stitch (beg V-st): Ch 6 (counts as dc and ch 3), dc in specified st or sp: beg V-st made.

V-stitch (V-st): Work (dDc, ch 3, dc) in specified st or sp: V-st made.

Increase V-stitch (inc V-st): (Dc, ch 3, dc, ch 3, dc) in specified st or sp: inc V-st made.

instructions continued on page 33

INSTRUCTIONS

Beginning at neck edge and working down, ch 50.

Row 1 (right side): Sc in 2nd ch from hook, *skip next 2 chs, shell in next ch, skip next 2 chs, sc in next ch; rep from * across: 8 shells and 9 sc; turn.

Row 2: Beg V-st in first sc; *sc in center dc of next shell, inc V-st in next sc, sc in center dc of next shell, V-st in next sc; rep from * across: 5 V-sts, 4 inc V-sts and 8 sc; ch 1, turn.

Row 3: Sc in first dc, shell in ch-3 sp of first V-st, (sc in next sc, shell in ch-3 of next inc V-st, sc in center dc of same inc V-st, shell in 2nd ch-3 sp of inc V-st, sc in next sc, shell in ch-3 of next V-st) 4 times; sc in 3rd ch of turning ch (part of beg V-st of Row 2.)

Row 4: Beg V-st in first sc, sc in center dc of first shell, (inc V-st in next sc, sc in center dc of next shell) 12 times, V-st in last sc: 2 V-sts, 12 inc V-sts and 13 sc; ch 1, turn.

Row 5: Sc in first dc, shell in ch-3 sp of first V-st, sc in next sc, (shell in first ch-3 sp of next inc V-st, sc in center dc of same inc V-st, shell in 2nd ch-3 sp of same inc V-st, sc in next sc) 12 times, shell in ch-3 sp of last V-st, sc in last dc: 26 shells and 27 sc; turn.

Row 6: Beg V-st in first sc; *sc in center dc of next shell, V-st in next sc; rep from * across: 27 V-sts and 26 sc; ch 1, turn.

Row 7: Sc in first dc; *shell in ch-3 sp of next V-st, sc in next sc; rep from * across: 27 shells and 28 sc; turn.

Rows 8 through 15: Rep Rows 6 and 7 four times more: 1 more V-st and 1 more sc on each even-numbered row; 1 more shell and 1 more sc on each odd-numbered row. At end of Row 15: 31 shells and 32 sc.

Row 16: Beg V-st in first sc, sc in center dc of next shell, (V-st in next sc, sc in center dc of next shell) 4 times; (inc V-st in next sc, sc in center dc of next shell, V-st in next sc, sc in center dc of next shell) 5 times; (V-st in next sc, sc in center dc of next shell) 3 times; (inc V-st in next sc, sc in center dc of next shell, V-st in next sc, sc in center dc of next shell) 5 times; (V-st in next sc, sc in center dc of next shell) 3 times, V-st in last sc: 22 V-sts, 10 inc V-sts and 31 sc; ch 1, turn.

Row 17: Sc in first dc, shell in ch-3 sp of each V-st, shell in first and 2nd ch-3 sps of each inc V-st, sc in each sc and sc in center dc of each inc V-st shell across, ending with sc in last dc: 42 shells and 43 sc; turn.

Rows 18 through 29: Work as for Rows 6 and 7 six times more; at end of Row 29: 48 shells and 49 sc. Finish off; weave in ends.

Five-Point Diamond Shawl

What woman doesn't love diamonds! Wrap her in them, and she's sure to be uplifted.

Skill Level: Intermediate

DESIGNED BY SHARI WHITE

Size
Approximately 64" wide x 58" long at center back point (163 cm x 147 cm)

Materials
Worsted weight yarn
[100% acrylic, 6 ounces, 315 yards (170 grams, 288 meters) per skein]
      3 skeins mauve

Note: *Photographed model made with Caron® Simply Soft® #9722 Plum Wine*

Size I (5.5 mm) crochet hook (or size required for gauge)

Gauge
Rows 1-4 = 7" wide x 3" high (18 cm x 8 cm)

Stitch Guide
Beginning V-Stitch Shell (beg V-st shell): (Sl st, ch 3, dc, ch 2, 2 dc) in specified ch-sp: beg V-st shell made.

V-Stitch Shell (V-st shell): Work (2 dc, ch 2, 2 dc) in same sp: V-st shell made.

Shell: Work 5 dc in same st or sp: shell made.

Large shell (lg shell): Work 7 dc in same st or sp: lg shell made.

Picot shell: Work 2 dc in specified st, ch 4, sl st in 4th ch from hook, 2 dc in same st as first 2 dc: picot shell made.

INSTRUCTIONS
Ch 12; join with sl st in first ch to form a ring.

Row 1 (wrong side): Beginning at center back of neck, ch 4 (counts as a dc and ch-1 sp), (dc in ring, ch 1) 7 times, dc in ring: 9 dc and 9 ch-1 sps; ch 6 (counts as dc and ch-3 sp on following row), turn. Do not join.

Row 2 (right side): (Dc in next dc, ch 3) 8 times, dc in 3rd ch of beg ch-5: 10 dc and 9 ch-3 sps; ch 1, turn.

Row 3: Work beg V-st shell in first ch-3 sp, (ch 3, dc in next ch-3 sp, ch 3, V-st shell in next ch-3 sp) 4 times, working last V-st shell in beg ch-6 sp: 5 V-st shells, 4 dc and 8 ch-3 sps; ch 2, turn.

Row 4: Work beg V-st shell in ch-2 sp of first V-st shell, (ch 3, dc in next ch-3 sp, dc in next dc, dc in next ch-3 sp, ch 3, V-st shell in ch-2 sp of next V-st shell) 4 times: 5 V-st shells, 4 groups of 3 dc and 8 ch-3 sps; ch 2, turn.

Row 5: Work beg V-st shell in ch-2 sp of first V-st shell, (ch 3, dc in next ch-3 sp, dc in next 3 dc, dc in next ch-3 sp, ch 3, V-st shell in ch-2 sp of next V-st shell) 4 times: 5 V-st shells, 4 groups of 5 dc and 8 ch-3 sps; ch 2, turn.

Row 6: Work beg V-st shell in ch-2 sp of first V-st shell, (ch 3, dc in next ch-3 sp, ch 3, skip next dc, dc in next 3 dc, skip next dc, ch 3, dc in next ch-3 sp, ch 3, V-st shell in ch-2 sp of next V-st shell) 4 times: 5 V-st shells, 4 groups of 3 dc, 8 dc and 16 ch-3 sps; ch 2, turn.

Row 7: Work beg V-st shell in ch-2 sp of first V-st shell, (ch 3, dc in next ch-3 sp, dc in next dc, dc in next ch-3 sp, ch 3, skip next dc, dc in next dc, skip next dc, ch 3, dc in next ch-3 sp, dc in next dc, dc in next ch-3 sp, ch

instructions continued on page 36

3, V-st shell in ch-2 sp of next V-st shell) 4 times: 5 V-st shells, 8 groups of 3 dc, 4 dc and 16 ch-3 sps; ch 2, turn.

Row 8: Work beg V-st shell in ch-2 sp of first V-st shell, (ch 3, dc in next ch-3 sp, dc in next 3 dc, dc in next ch-3 sp, ch 5, dc in next ch-3 sp, dc in next 3 dc, dc in next ch-3 sp, ch 3, V-st shell in ch-2 sp of next V-st shell) 4 times: 5 V-st shells, 8 groups of 5 dc, 4 ch-5 sps and 8 ch-3 sps; ch 2, turn.

Row 9: Work beg V-st shell in ch-2 sp of first V-st shell, (ch 3, dc in next ch-3 sp; *ch 3, skip next dc, dc in next 3 dc, skip next dc, ch 3, dc in next ch-sp; rep from * across to next V-st shell; ch 3, V-st shell in ch-2 sp of next V-st shell) 4 times: 5 V-st shells, 8 groups of 3 dc, 12 dc and 24 ch-3 sps; ch 2, turn.

Row 10: Work beg V-st shell in ch-2 sp of first V-st shell, work [(ch 3, dc in next ch-3 sp, dc in next dc, dc in next ch-3 sp; *ch 3, skip next dc, dc in next dc, skip next dc, ch 3, dc in next ch-3 sp, dc in next dc, dc in next ch-3 sp; rep from * across to next V-st shell; ch 3, V-st shell in ch-2 sp of next V-st shell)] 4 times: 5 V-st shells, 12 groups of 3 dc, 8 dc and 24 ch-3 sps; ch 2, turn.

Row 11: Work beg V-st shell in ch-2 sp of first V-st shell, work [(ch 3, dc in next ch-3 sp, dc in next 3 dc, dc in next ch-3 sp; *ch 5, dc in next ch-3 sp, dc in next 3 dc, dc in next ch-3 sp; rep from * across to next V-st shell; ch 3, V-st shell in ch-2 sp of next V-st shell)] 4 times: 5 V-st shells, 12 groups of 5 dc, 8 ch-5 sps and 8 ch-3 sps; ch 2, turn.

Row 12: Work beg V-st shell in ch-2 sp of first V-st shell, work [(ch 3, dc in next ch-3 sp; *ch 3, skip next dc, dc in next 3 dc, skip next dc, ch 3, dc in next ch-sp; rep from * across to next V-st shell; ch 3, V-st shell in ch-2 sp of next V-st shell)] 4 times: 5 V-st shells, 12 groups of 3 dc, 16 dc and 32 ch-3 sps; ch 2, turn.

Row 13: Work beg V-st shell in ch-2 sp of first V-st shell, work [(ch 3, dc in next ch-3 sp, dc in next dc, dc in next ch-3 sp; *ch 3, skip next dc, dc in next dc, skip next dc, ch 3, dc in next ch-3 sp, dc in next dc, dc in next

ch-3 sp; rep from * across to next V-st shell; ch 3, V-st shell in ch-2 sp of next V-st shell)] 4 times: 5 V-st shells, 16 groups of 3 dc, 12 dc and 32 ch-3 sps; ch 2, turn.

Row 14: Work beg V-st shell in ch-2 sp of first V-st shell, work [(ch 3, dc in next ch-3 sp, dc in next 3 dc, dc in next ch-3 sp; *ch 5, dc in next ch-3 sp, dc in next 3 dc, dc in next ch-3 sp; rep from * across to next V-st shell; ch 3, V-st shell in ch-2 sp of next V-st shell)] 4 times: 5 V-st shells, 16 groups of 5 dc, 12 ch-5 sps and 8 ch-3 sps; ch 2, turn.

Rows 15 and 16: Rep Rows 9 and 10: 8 more groups of 3 dc, 8 more dc and 16 more ch-3 sps than previous rep of Rows 9 and 10.

Row 17: Rep Row 11: 8 more groups of 5 dc and 8 more ch-5 sps than previous rep of Row 11.

Rows 18 and 19: Rep Rows 12 and 13: 8 more groups of 3 dc, 8 more dc and 16 more ch-3 sps than previous rep of Rows 12 and 13.

Row 20: Rep Row 14: 8 more groups of 5 dc and 8 more ch-5 sps than previous rep of Row 14.

Rows 21-41: Rep Rows 15-20, 3 times more, then rep Rows 15-17 once more. At end of Row 41: 5 V-st shells, 52 groups of 5 dc, 48 ch-5 sps and 8 ch-3 sps.

EDGING

Row 1 (right side): Work beg V-st shell in ch-2 sp of first V-st shell, ch 3; (*sc in next ch-sp, skip next 2 dc, shell in next dc, skip next 2 dc; rep from * across to next V-st shell**; shell in ch-2 sp of next V-st shell) 3 times; rep from * to ** once; sc in last ch-sp, ch 3, V-st shell in ch-2 sp of last V-st shell: 2 V-st shells, 55 shells, 56 sc and 2 ch-3 sps; ch 2, turn.

Row 2: Work beg V-st shell in ch-2 sp of first V-st shell, ch 3; *sc in next sc, skip next 2 dc, lg shell in next dc, skip next 2 dc, sc in next sc; rep from * across to last V-st shell; sc in next sc, ch 3, V-st shell in ch-2 sp of last V-st shell: 2 V-st shells, 55 lg shells, 56 sc and 2 ch-3 sps; ch 2, turn.

Row 3: Work beg V-st shell in ch-2 sp of first V-st shell, ch 3; *sc in next sc, ch 3, skip next 3 dc, picot shell in next dc, skip next 3 dc, ch 3; repeat from * across to last V-st shell; sc in next sc, ch 3, V-st shell in ch-2 sp of last V-st shell: 2 V-st shells, 55 picot shells, 56 sc and 112 ch-3 sps. Fasten off.

Weave in all ends. Block shawl, if desired.

A Shawl for a Little Miss

What a fun way to let a darling girl know how much she is loved.

Skill Level: Easy

DESIGNED BY JEAN LEINHAUSER

Size
Approximately 48" wide x 17" long
(122 cm x 43 cm)

Materials
Bulky weight yarn
[80% acrylic, 20% nylon, 3 ounces, 155 yards
(85 grams, 141 meters) per skein]
       3 skeins rose

Note: *Photographed model made with Caron®
Dazzleaire #0001 Summer Rose.*

Size K (6.5 mm) crochet hook (or size required for gauge)

Gauge
11 dc and 5 dc rows = 4" (10 cm)

INSTRUCTIONS
Ch 49.

Row 1 (wrong side): Dc in 4th ch from hook (skipped chs count as first dc), dc in next ch, (ch 1, skip next ch, dc in next 4 chs) 8 times, ch 1, skip next ch, dc in last 3 chs: 38 dc and 9 ch-1 sps; ch 3 (counts as dc on next row now and throughout), turn.

Row 2 (right side): Dc in next 2 dc, (ch 1, skip next ch-1 sp, dc in next dc, 2 dc in next dc, dc in next 2 dc) 8 times, ch 1, skip last ch-1 sp, dc in last 3 dc: 46 dc and 9 ch-1 sps; ch 3, turn.

Row 3: Dc in next 2 dc, (ch 1, skip next ch-1 sp, dc in next dc, 2 dc in next dc, dc in each dc across to next ch-1 sp) 8 times, ch 1, skip last ch-1 sp, dc in last 3 dc: 54 dc and 9 ch-1 sps; ch 3, turn.

Rows 4-10: Rep Row 3, 7 times more: 8 more dc in each row. At end of Row 10: 110 dc and 9 ch-1 sps.

Row 11: Dc in next 2 dc; *ch 1, skip next ch-1 sp, dc in next dc, (ch 1, skip next dc, dc in next dc) 6 times; rep from * 7 times more; ch 1, skip last ch-1 sp, dc in last 3 dc: 62 dc and 57 ch-1 sps; ch 3, turn.

Rows 12-18: Dc in next 2 dc; *ch 1, skip next ch-1 sp, dc in next dc; rep from * across to last ch-1 sp; ch 1, skip last ch-1 sp, dc in last 3 dc; ch 3, turn.

Row 19: Dc in next 2 dc; *2 dc in next ch-1 sp, dc in next dc; rep from * across to last 2 dc; dc in last 2 dc: 176 dc; ch 3, turn.

Row 20: Dc in next dc; *2 dc in next dc, dc in next dc; rep from * across: 263 dc; ch 3, turn.

Row 21: Dc in next dc and in each dc across; ch 1, turn.

Row 22: Sc in first dc; *ch 3, skip next dc, sc in next dc; rep from * across: 131 ch-3 sps. Finish off; weave in ends.

TOP EDGING AND COLLAR

Row 1: With right side facing, working in free lps of foundation chs, join with sc in first ch, sc in next 2 chs, sc in next ch-1 sp; *sc in next 4 chs, sc in next ch-1 sp; rep from * across to last 3 chs; sc in last 3 chs: 47 sc. Finish off; weave in ends.

Row 2: With right side facing, join with sl st in first sc; *ch 45 (for tie), sc in 2nd ch from hook and in next 43 chs**; sc in each sc across Row 1; rep from * to ** once; join with sl st in edge of last sc on Row 1: 135 sc. Finish off; weave in ends.

A WRAP FOR BABY BLUE EYES

Even the youngest will turn tears into smiles when covered with prayers and a baby wrap.

Skill Level: Easy

DESIGNED BY MARY ANN FRITS

Size

Fits 2T-4T

Materials

Bulky weight yarn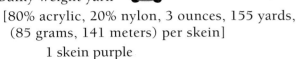
[80% acrylic, 20% nylon, 3 ounces, 155 yards,
(85 grams, 141 meters) per skein]
1 skein purple

Note: *Photographed model made with Caron, Dazz-elaire #0003 Thistle*

Size J/10 (6 mm) crochet hook or size required for gauge

Gauge

6 sts = 2"

INSTRUCTIONS

Ch 56; being carefully not to twist ch, join with sl st in first ch.

Rnd 1 (right side): Ch 3 (counts as a dc on this and following rnds), *sk next 2 chs, dc in each of next 2 chs, in next ch work (dc, ch 3, dc), dc in each of next 2 chs, rep from * around, end last rep with dc in last ch, join in 3rd ch of beg ch-3.

Rnd 2: Sl st in each of next 2 dc, ch 3, dc in next dc, *in next ch-3 sp work (dc, ch 3, dc), dc in each of next 2 dc, sk next 2 dc**, dc in each of next 2 dc, rep from * around, ending last rep at **, join in 3rd ch of beg ch-3.

Rnd 3: Sl st in next dc, ch 3, dc in next dc, *in next ch-3 sp work (2 dc, ch 3, 2 dc), dc in each of next 2 dc, sk next 2 dc**, dc in each of next 2 dc, rep from * around, ending last rep at **, join in 3rd ch of beg ch-3.

Rnd 4: Sl st in next dc, ch 3, dc in each of next 2 dc, *in next ch-3 sp work (dc, ch 3, dc), dc in each of next 3 dc, sk next 2 dc**, dc in each of next 3 dc, rep from * around, ending last rep at **, join in 3rd ch of beg ch-3.

instructions continued on page 42

Rnd 5: Sl st in next dc, ch 3, dc in each of next 2 dc, *in next ch-3 sp work (2 dc, ch 3, 2 dc), dc in each of next 3 dc, sk next 2 dc**, dc in each of next 3 dc, rep from * around, ending last rep at **, join in 3rd ch of beg ch-3.

Rnd 6: Sl st in next dc, ch 3, dc in each of next 3 dc, *in next ch-3 sp work (dc, ch 3, dc), dc in each of next 4 dc, sk next 2 dc**, dc in each of next 4 dc, rep from * around, ending last rep at **, join in 3rd ch of beg ch-3.

Rnd 7: Sl st in next dc, ch 3, dc in each of next 3 dc, *in next ch-3 sp work (2 dc, ch 3, 2 dc), dc in each of next 4 dc, sk next 2 dc**, dc in each of next 4 dc, rep from * around, ending last rep at **, join in 3rd ch of beg ch-3.

Rnd 8: Sl st in next dc, ch 3, dc in each of next 4 dc, *in next ch-3 sp work (2 dc, ch 3, 2 dc), dc in each of next 5 dc, sk next 2 dc**, dc in each of next 5 dc, rep from * around, ending last rep at **, join in 3rd ch of beg ch-3.

Rnd 9: Sl st in next dc, ch 3, dc in each of next 5 dc, *in next ch-3 sp work (dc, ch 4, sl st in 3rd ch from hook for picot, ch 1, dc), dc in each of next 6 dc, sk next 2 dc**, dc in each of next 6 dc, rep from * around, ending last rep at **, join in 3rd ch of beg ch-3. Finish off; weave in ends.

GENERAL INSTRUCTIONS

Abbreviations and Symbols

Crochet patterns are written in a special shorthand which is used so that instructions don't take up too much space. They sometimes seem confusing, but once you learn them, you'll have no trouble following them.

These are Abbreviations

Beg	beginning
BL	back loop
BLO	back loop only
Cl(s)	cluster(s)
Ch(s)	chain(s)
Cm	centimeter
Cont	continue
Dc	double crochet
Dc dec	double crochet decrease
Dec	decrease
Esc	extended single crochet
Fig	figure
FL	front loop
Hdc	half double crochet
Inc	increase(ing)
Lg shell	large shell
Long sc	long single croche
Lp(s)	loop(s)
Lp St	loop stitch
LscCl	long single crochet cluster
Mm	millimeter
Oz	ounce
Patt	pattern
Prev	previous
Rem	remaining
Rep	repeat(ing)
Rev	reverse
Rev sc	reverse single crochet
Rnd(s)	round(s)
Sc	single crochet
sc dec	single crochet decrease
Sl st	slip stitch
Sp(s)	space(s)
St(s)	stitch(es)
Tog	together
Tr	triple crochet
V-st	V-stitch
YO	yarn over hook

These are Standard Symbols

* An asterisk (or double asterisks**) in a pattern row, indicates a portion of instructions to be used more than once. For instance, "rep from * three times" means that after working the instructions once, you must work them again three times for a total of 4 times in all.

† A dagger (or double daggers ††) indicates that those instructions will be repeated again later in the same row or round.

: The number of stitches after a colon tells you the number of stitches you will have when you have completed the row or round.

( ) Parentheses enclose instructions which are to be worked the number of times following the parentheses. For instance, "(ch 1, sc, ch1) 3 times" means that you will chain one, work one sc, and then chain again three times for a total of six chains and three scs.

Parentheses often set off or clarify a group of stitches to be worked into the same space of stitch. For instance, "(dc, ch2, dc) in corner sp".

[ ] Brackets and ( ) parentheses are also used to give you additional information.

Gauge

This is probably the most important aspect of crocheting!

Gauge simply means the number of stitches per inch, and the number of rows per inch that result from a specified yarn worked with a hook in a specified size. But since everyone crochets differently—some loosely, some tightly, some in between—the measurements of individual work can vary greatly, even when the crocheters use the same pattern and the same size yarn and hook.

If you don't work to the gauge specified in the pattern, your shawl will never be the correct size, and you may not have enough yarn to finish your project. The hook size given in the instructions is merely a guide and should never be used without a gauge swatch.

To make a gauge swatch, crochet a piece that is about 4" square, using the suggested hook and the number of stitches given in the pattern. Measure your swatch. If the number of stitches is fewer than those listed in the pattern, try making another swatch with a smaller hook. If the number of stitches is more than is called for in the pattern, try making another swatch with a larger hook. It is your responsibility to make sure you achieve the gauge specified in the pattern.

Terms

Front Loop – This is the loop toward you at the top of the crochet stitch.

Back Loop – This is the loop away from you at the top of the crochet stitch.

Post – This is the vertical part of the crochet stitch

Join – This means to join with a sl st unless another stitch is specified.

Finish Off – This means to end your piece by pulling the cut yarn end through the last loop remaining on the hook. This will prevent the work from unraveling.

Continue in pattern as established – This means to follow the pattern stitch as it has been set up, working any increases or decreases in such a way that the pattern remains the same as it was established.

Work even – This means that the work is continued in the pattern as established without increasing or decreasing.

Crochet Hooks

Buying a crochet hook can be confusing because of the way crochet hooks are marked. Different manufacturers use different markings—some use a letter system, others use a numbering system. The most accurate way to choose a hook is to go by the millimeter (mm) sizing, which refers to the hook's diameter. Here is a guide from the Craft Yarn Council.

Mm Size	Letter Size	Number Size
2.25 mm	B	1
2.75 mm	C	2
3.25 mm	D	3
3.50 mm	E	4
3.75 mm	F	5
4.00 mm	G	6
4.50 mm	—	7
5.00 mm	H	8
5.50 mm	I	9
6.00 mm	J	10
6.50 mm	K	10½
8.00 mm	L	11
9.00 mm	M or N	13
10.00 mm	N	15
12.00 mm	O	—
15.00 mm	P	—
16.00 mm	Q	—
19.00 mm	S	—

Crochet Terminology

The patterns in this book have been written using the crochet terminology that is used in the United States. Terms which may have different equivalents in other parts of the world are listed below.

United States	International
Double crochet (dc)	treble crochet (tr)
Gauge	tension
Half double crochet (hdc)	half treble crochet (htr)
Single crochet	double crochet
Skip	miss
Slip stitch	single crochet
Triple crochet (tr)	double treble crochet (dtr)